Dedication

This book is for all of the men in my life who know me and love me anyway. My dad is a good draftsman and an innovative thinker. I have inherited his love of precision and his curiosity. Thanks, Pop! My creativity is uniquely mine but is tolerated and encouraged by my husband, Chris. Our sons, Randy and Bryan, think my quilts are awesome. Thanks, guys!

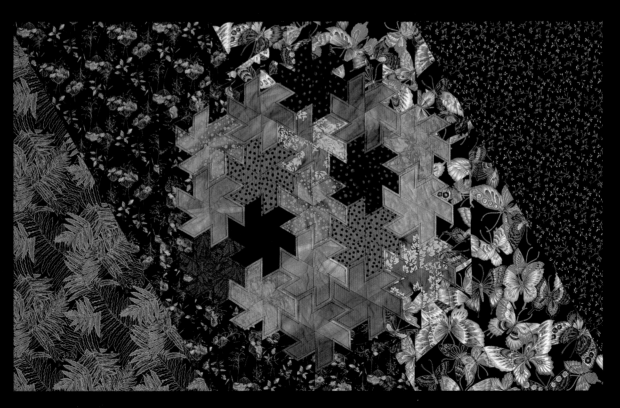

Contents

Preface

I thank God for all things, including insomnia. It came on with menopause, and fortunately it is becoming infrequent again. But when it happens, I don't mind. I have spent many nocturnal hours playing with geometric shapes in my mind. I can design quilts by the dozen as I'm dozin'!

One night I tackled the question I had been avoiding for a long time: What can I do with hexagons? Given my love of tessellated shapes and the success of my earlier book *Square Dance*, the answer was obvious: Just sew them together, then cut them up and re-sew them as I had done so many times with squares.

The drawback I imagined is that most quilters hope to avoid set-in seams. When you sew hexagons together, set-in seams are required at every corner. Ouch! But as I visualized my unconventional construction technique—cutting, sewing, cutting again, and sewing again—I saw that the first hexagons would be so large that piecing them would not be difficult at all. Having taken care of the hard part, the rest of the piecing became quite easy in my mind.

Once again, I threw off the blankets in the middle of the night, groped for my robe and glasses, and headed off down the hall to my sewing room (my long-suffering husband is accustomed to this by now). A few samples later, my vision was reality and I'd proved that the technique would work.

So, here I am again, ready to introduce you to an easier way to stitch together pieces that were once difficult and time consuming. I hope you will find as much pleasure in this technique as I have had in bringing it to you. Happy stitching!

Introduction

This book is about taking a hexagon and turning it into a tessellated shape. *Tessellated*. Now, there's a big word, but it has a simple explanation. Tessellated shapes are simply motifs that interlock. It sounds complex, and it can be, but with the technique I've devised and presented in this book you'll be able to turn fabric hexagons into exciting, unconventional shapes that seem to swirl freely while paradoxically interlocked with their neighbors.

By now you're probably eager to understand the basic technique. The condensed version is that you sew a specified number of hexagons together to make one large piece. Then you cut triangles from the large piece and sew them together to create what I call "swirligigs." The entire process is explained in detail in "General Instructions" on pages 9–15. There you'll find the specific instructions you'll need to make any of the quilts in the book, so be sure you understand the chapter and make the sample project that accompanies it before you delve into the project chapter.

When you are ready for the projects, on pages 18–63, I suggest you start with one of the smaller, simpler quilts, such as "Swirligig Wreath" or "Line Dance." Then, once you have a feel for cutting and sewing the pieces together, move on to any of the others. Many of the projects include a design sheet to help you create your own pattern. Use the quilts photographed for inspiration, but by all means, mix things up and let the swirligigs land where you want them. Just remember to recalculate your batting and backing requirements if you make significant changes in the size of the quilt.

With these thoughts in mind, go start a pot of steaming coffee and settle in for some nontraditional patchwork. You'll soon be creating amazingly intricate-looking patchwork designs in a few simple steps. Shhh! Don't tell anyone it was easy. Let them think you're a genius!

Fabric and Equipment

Fabric

The tessellating technique used in this book requires more yardage than traditional patchwork techniques, so don't skimp when buying your fabrics. You will need all of the yardage called for in the instructions. The upside is that after the second cutting you will have some nifty hexagons left over, perfect for another quilt of equal beauty.

If you have done any sewing, whether a garment or a quilt, no doubt you know the importance of fabric grain. My technique virtually ignores the existence of grain and bias in fabric, which is not usually a good idea since woven fabrics have different properties depending on the direction of the grain. So here are a few hints to help you avoid some pretty ugly problems.

- Use good-quality, 100 percent–cotton fabrics. The best way to assure quality is simply to pay for it! Patronize your local quilt shop, where you'll find first-run, high-quality fabrics that will not shrink out of shape when the quilt is washed. A fabric with even a small percentage of polyester will not work with this technique.

- For the focal fabrics in these designs, small-scale prints, solids, and hand-dyed fabrics work best. For the backgrounds, medium-scale, busy prints usually work well.

- Nondirectional prints work best for the hexagons. Don't rule out directional prints entirely, though, as they can prove very interesting. If you do choose a directional print, just be sure to make a sample before you piece all the hexagons together and find out they don't work quite the way you thought they would.

- Do not prewash your fabrics. The sizing that has been added to them will improve the way they handle.

- Steam press your fabrics before cutting out the pieces; you want any shrinkage to occur before cutting rather than after. Add a bit more starch or sizing as you steam press if the fabrics don't have as much body as you'd like.

- Handle all cut pieces carefully, especially those with bias edges. Be careful not to stretch these edges. They are not elastic and will not snap back.

- Sew on a machine that handles bias edges well, without stretching them. Use a new needle. Lighten up the pressure of the presser foot if possible.

- After the initial steam pressing of your uncut fabrics, use water in your iron only when all edges are enclosed in seams. Damp fabric is easily distorted.

- Relax! The tension in your body will travel through your hands and into your work. If you are not relaxed, your patchwork will show it.

Equipment

If you don't already have the following supplies on hand, they should be readily available at your local fabric store or office-supply store.

Ironing supplies. As with any sewn project, pressing is key to a successful finished product. No fancy equipment is needed, just an iron that has variable heat settings and that can be used with or without steam. If you do not have a steam feature on your iron, a spray bottle filled with water can be used to spritz the fabric before ironing. For the ironing surface, a traditional ironing board or a terry-cloth towel placed on a heatproof surface is all you need.

Marking tools. For tracing patterns onto template plastic, I prefer a fine-point, permanent black marker. Laundry markers or the fabric markers commonly found at quilt shops work well. For tracing around templates onto fabric, you can generally use the same markers—just test yours first on a scrap of your fabric to make sure it doesn't bleed. Tailor's chalk is excellent on dark fabrics. An ordinary sharp pencil is another option.

Paper punch. I find that a hand punch that makes a hole one-sixteenth inch in diameter is very helpful. Use it to mark corner dots on plastic templates, as designated by dots on the patterns. You should be able to find a small-hole punch in the craft department of your local fabric store, discount retailer, or office-supply store. If you cannot, a small-size leather punch, darning needle, or other sharp object can be used.

Scissors. Remember the dressmaker's shears you used before the rotary cutter was invented? My hexagon patchwork is not rotary cut, so if you've been out of touch with your scissors, I'll tell you right now that you're going to become good friends again. Get them sharpened if they are dull. It's best to use a different pair of scissors for cutting through template plastic.

Template plastic. Lots of different products are available for making templates, but clear or translucent plastic is essential for this technique. It comes in 14" x 20" sheets that are easily cut with scissors, and is available at most quilt shops.

General Instructions

Most of the quilts in this book follow the same basic method: sewing hexagons together, cutting them into triangles, arranging the triangles into rows, and sewing the rows together. Refer to this section as you construct each project.

Making the Templates

The patterns you need to create your own templates are provided for each project. All of the patterns are full size, but some are too large to be given complete on a page. In these cases, only a portion of the pattern is given. Follow the instructions below to make complete templates.

For some of the projects, after cutting one set of pieces with a given template, you will cut the outer portion of the template away to make a second template. If you wish to save your templates for later projects, just trace the outer and inner templates separately.

To make a template from a complete pattern:

1. Place a piece of template plastic over the pattern.
2. Using a permanent marker, trace the perimeter of the shape along the solid lines. Then transfer any inner solid and dashed lines and corner dots onto the plastic. Mark the grain line, if given.
3. Label the template with the template letter and quilt name. Mark "This side up" on the template to prevent you from flipping it over.
4. Cut out the template on the perimeter lines. Do not add seam allowances.

5. Use a hand punch or other tool to make small holes in the template where indicated by the corner dots.

To make a template from a partial pattern:

1. Place a piece of template plastic over the partial pattern. Position the plastic to allow room to complete the pattern.
2. Using a permanent marker, trace the perimeter of the shape, including the red line on which you'll rotate the template plastic. Then transfer any corner dots onto the plastic. Mark the grain line, if given.
3. If one-half of the pattern is given, rotate the template plastic 180° until the template half butts up to the pattern half along the center line. Trace the rest of the perimeter along the solid lines, and transfer any corner dots.

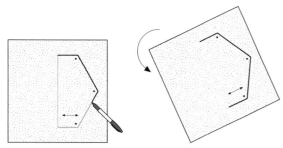

Trace half of pattern.   Rotate template plastic 180°.

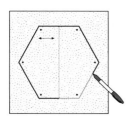

Trace other half of pattern.

4. If one-third of the pattern is given, rotate the template plastic 120° until the template third butts up to the pattern third along the rotation line. Trace the perimeter of the shape along the solid lines, and transfer any

corner dots. Then rotate the template plastic another 120° and finish tracing.

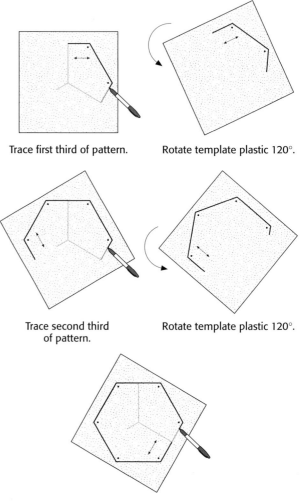

Trace first third of pattern.   Rotate template plastic 120°.

Trace second third of pattern.   Rotate template plastic 120°.

Trace final third of pattern.

5. Complete the template by referring to steps 3–5 on pages 9–10.

Cutting Out the Hexagons

For the quilts in this book, most of the pieces are cut with templates, but some pieces, such as borders and binding, are cut before the template pieces. The individual project directions will indicate when these should be cut first.

While this new construction technique employs old-fashioned templates, they do not have to be used in old-fashioned ways. Any time you need to cut many (fifty, seventy, even a hundred or more) hexagons from fabric, I encourage you to fold or stack, wrong side up, as many layers as you can comfortably cut through with your scissors. Then, following the grain line if marked on the template, place the template on the stack of fabric and mark around it on the top layer only. Remove the template, and cut through all the layers at once. Use the template again to mark corner dots on each individual piece. After a little practice, you may be able to "eyeball" the corner dots instead of depending on markings. When you develop this level of confidence, you may forgo the marking of corner dots with my blessing. You may also want to mark one of the straight-grain edges on each piece with a straight pin.

Piecing the Hexagons

Once your hexagons are cut out, you're ready to piece them together.

- Place two hexagons right sides together. You can improve the overall stability of your patchwork by matching a straight-grain edge with a bias-grain edge whenever possible.

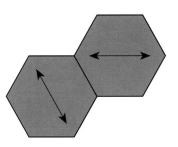

- To stitch the hexagons together, first align the marked corner dots at both ends of the seam. Begin each seam by backstitching one or two stitches to the first dot, then, using a ¼" seam allowance, stitch forward all the way to the dot at the end of the seam; back-

stitch two or three stitches from the end dot. Be careful to stitch between the dots, never beyond them. Clip threads.

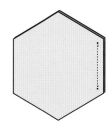

- Always stitch all the way to a corner dot to avoid either gaps where stitches do not meet or little pleats where pieces shift out of alignment. To avoid puckered corners and seams that will not lie flat, never stitch beyond a dot, even by one little stitch.

- Stitch one seam at a time, cutting the threads between seams. There is no way to chain these pieces through your machine quickly, so just be patient.

- It makes no difference whatsoever which seam you begin with or in which order you sew the seams. Follow whatever order you wish unless the instructions specify otherwise. Kind of liberating, isn't it!

- When setting in a third hexagon where two have already been joined, align the corner dots, then hold the pieces up and let the extra fabric drop. Its weight will gently pull the seams into perfect alignment and produce crisp, perfect corners. Even the unpressed seam allowances fall out of the way, allowing you to stitch unhindered all the way to the corner dots. Now you know the secret of perfect set-in seams!

- Exception: There is no need to match dots and backstitch from dots at the outside edges of the quilt top. Just sew to the edges of the fabric.

Cutting Out the Triangles and Forming the Swirligigs

Once you've pieced all the hexagons together, it's time to cut them apart. Here's how to do it.

1. Create the specified triangle template. For some of the projects, you will cut away portions of the template used to mark the hexagons, leaving a triangle template. For other projects, the triangle pattern is given separately.

2. Working on the right side of the pieced hexagon, place the center of the triangle template over any point where three seams meet. Rotate the template until the dashed lines marked on the template lie directly over the three seams. Using a fine-point permanent marker, tailor's chalk, or a sharp pencil, trace around the template. Repeat the tracing process, centering the triangle template over every place where three seams meet. Be sure you do not flip the template over as you are tracing the triangles; reversing the template will throw you into total confusion!

    It is entirely possible, even probable, that at first some of the traced triangles will not fit perfectly next to their neighboring triangles. They may overlap slightly or there may be a small gap between them. When this happens, recheck the position of your template; make sure that the three dashed

lines all lie directly over seam lines. When the lines are matched up, trace around the template. Those little irregularities will not make any difference in your final project.

3. Cut out all of the triangles, and lay them on the work surface in exactly the same position they had before cutting. If you come to lines that overlap slightly or do not quite meet, just cut midway between mismatched lines, and those little differences will disappear into the seam allowances when the pieces are stitched together again.

4. Carefully rotate the six triangles that formed one of the original hexagons so that the six points that share the same fabric meet in the center. That hexagon has been magically transformed into a swirligig!

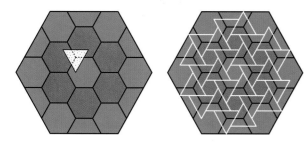

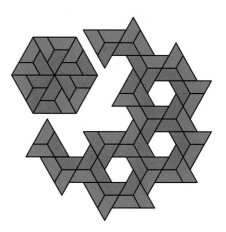

5. Rearrange the remaining triangles in the same manner, matching the six points of common fabric at the center of each swirligig. Step back and inspect your new creation of spinning shapes!

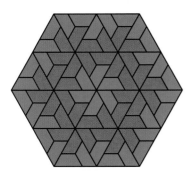

Sewing the Swirligigs

Now that you've created the swirligigs, you're ready to stitch them together.

1. Divide the triangles into rows.
2. Stitch the triangles in each row together. Refer to "Pressing Matters" on page 15 to press the seams.

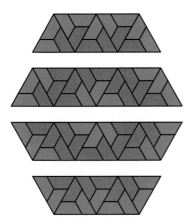

3. Stitch the rows together. Refer to "Pressing Matters" on page 15 to press the stitched piece.

Sisters: An Introductory Project

It only takes two to tessellate! Here is a quick and easy project that will enable you to see how big, clunky hexagons are transformed into the moving, interlocking shapes I call swirligigs. Using fusible web in the project eliminates the need to sew seams and allows you to concentrate on the patchwork shapes. Substituting paper for fabric is another easy way to learn the basics of this technique. When your piece is finished, use it to cover a special notebook or a gift box.

Materials

All yardage is based on 42"-wide fabric unless otherwise stated.

6" x 6" square *each* of 2 coordinating solids or small prints

½ yd. background fabric

½ yd. paper-backed fusible web

Template plastic

Cutting

From the background fabric, cut:

    1 rectangle, 10½" x 15"

From the fusible web, cut:

    2 squares, each 6" x 6"

    1 rectangle, 10" x 14½"

Make the Template

1. Place template plastic over pattern A on page 68.
2. Using a permanent marker, trace around the perimeter of the hexagon, then transfer the inner solid and dashed lines to the plastic.
3. Cut out the template on the perimeter lines.

Cut Out and Assemble the Hexagons

1. Trace the perimeter of template A onto the paper side of each 6" fusible web square. Following the manufacturer's instructions, fuse each fusible web square to the wrong side of a 6" fabric square. Cut out the hexagons on the marked lines.
2. Fold the background fabric rectangle into fourths to find the center point; pinch a small crease into the fabric to mark the center. Remove the paper backing from the hexagons. Using the center point as a reference, place the 2 hexagons, sides touching, in the center of the background rectangle. Follow the manufacturer's instructions to fuse the hexagons in place.

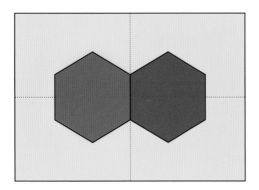

3. Follow the manufacturer's instructions to fuse the 10" x 14½" rectangle of fusible web to the wrong side of the background fabric piece. Let cool. Remove the paper backing.

Cut Out the Triangles and Form the Swirligigs

1. Modify template A by cutting along the inner solid lines, leaving the triangle that was inside the hexagon.
2. Place the background fabric right side up on the work surface. Place the triangle template directly over any corner of either of the 2 hexagons, matching the template center to the point of the hexagon. Rotate the template until 2 of the 3 dashed lines align with the outer edges of the hexagon. Use a sharp pencil to mark lightly around the template. Repeat for all of the corners of both hexagons. You should have 10 triangles.

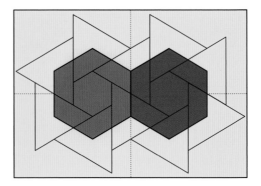

3. Cut out all of the triangles, and lay them on the work surface in exactly the same position they had before cutting.

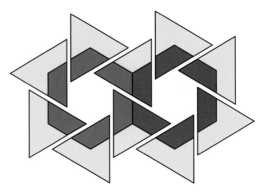

Pressing Matters

Proper pressing techniques make all the difference when working with set-in seams and bias grains. The steps below will help ensure success as you stitch your projects together.

1. Stitch all of the hexagons together as instructed for each project.

2. Lay the stitched piece on your ironing board with the wrong side facing up.

3. Using a dry iron on a medium setting, press all of the seams either open or to one side. I prefer open, but it takes more time. If you choose to press them to one side, do it methodically. Spiral seams around one set-in point, then do a reverse spiral around the next set-in point.

4. When all of the seams have been pressed, turn the stitched piece to the right side and steam press with the iron on a hot setting. Allow the piece to cool before cutting out the required triangle pieces.

5. After the triangles have been sewn into rows, use a dry iron on a medium-hot setting to press the seams either open or to one side. If you choose to press the seams to one side, be careful to alternate the direction from row to row to reduce bulk.

6. Stitch the rows together, and press the seams either open or to one side, using a dry iron on a medium-hot setting.

7. Steam press the quilt top from the right side, using a hot iron.

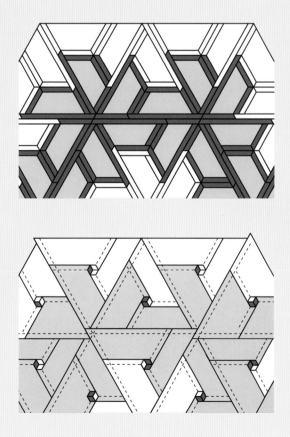

4. Carefully rotate the 6 triangles that formed one of the original hexagons so that the 6 points that share the same fabric meet in the center. Visualize the lens of a camera closing and you will see how the triangles come together. You have now created your first swirligig!

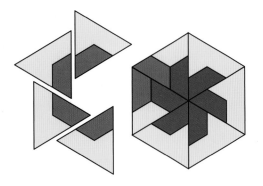

5. Reposition the remaining triangles so the points of the second hexagon meet the points of the same color on the first swirligig. You now have 2 swirligigs.

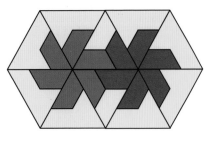

Finish the Project

1. Transfer all of the triangles to the center of the remaining piece of background fabric, keeping them in position. Place them close together so that no background fabric shows between the triangles.
2. Follow the manufacturer's instructions to fuse the triangles in place.
3. Trim the edges of the background fabric to the desired size.

Designing Your Own Quilt

For many of the projects in this book, a design sheet is provided so you can arrange the hexagons to your liking. There's no reason you have to make the quilt exactly as shown in the photograph, but it's okay if you do.

The design sheets provided will make quilts the size shown. But size too can be altered if you feel you've got the hang of the technique and want to start experimenting. Just add or delete hexagons on the design sheet. It's that easy.

Use the design sheet to determine where to put the swirligigs. Every hexagon on the design sheet represents either a swirligig or background fabric. Decide which fabric(s) you want to be the focus (swirligigs) and which fabric(s) you want to be the background. From those fabrics, cut hexagons to the size of those on the design sheet (note that some of the hexagons along the outer edges are incomplete). Then just move the fabric hexagons around the design sheet until you're pleased with the arrangement.

Feel free to change your composition. For example, you may want to cut a large area of background as one piece and not as individual hexagons (see "Epic Changes" on page 34, and "Windmills of My Mind" on page 40). Go ahead, do it! Just be sure to surround each swirligig with six other hexagons, of either background fabric or focus fabric, to ensure that your swirligig will still have all six of its arms when the cutting is done.

Quilt Projects

Swirligig Wreath
Designed by Martha Thompson, 2001, Seattle, Washington, 25" x 22".
Pieced and quilted by Donna DeShazo.

Swirligig Wreath

Just two fabrics are all you need to make this dynamic wreath-shaped design that's perfect for any holiday. This quick little quilt has many uses, too: make one as a table decoration, or make several as generous-size place mats; hang it in a small place to add a festive touch to your holiday decorating; wrap it around a bottle of wine and give it as a hostess gift; or use it to cover hot rolls in a round basket. I'm sure you'll think of even more uses as you construct this delightful little quilt.

Materials

All yardage is based on 42"-wide fabric unless otherwise stated.

⅞ yd. print for wreath and binding

⅞ yd. coordinating print for background and borders

⅞ yd. fabric for backing

26" x 29" rectangle of batting

Template plastic

Cutting

From the wreath fabric, cut:

    2 strips, each 2½" x 42", for binding

From the background fabric, cut:

    6 strips, each 2½" x 16", for borders

Cut Out and Assemble the Hexagons

1. Referring to "Making the Templates" on page 9, trace pattern B on page 69 onto template plastic. Mark the template and cut it out.

2. Using template B and referring to "Cutting Out the Hexagons" on page 10, cut 6 hexagons from the remaining wreath fabric and 10 hexagons from the remaining background fabric.

3. Cut 3 of the background hexagons in half as shown.

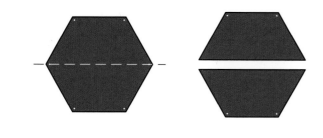

4. Arrange the wreath hexagons, the whole background hexagons, and the halved background hexagons as shown at left. Refer to "Piecing the Hexagons" on page 11 to stitch the hexagons together.

5. Refer to "Pressing Matters" on page 15 to press the stitched piece.

Cut Out the Triangles and Form the Swirligigs

1. Modify template B by cutting along the inner solid lines, leaving the triangle that was inside the hexagon.

2. Working on the right side of the stitched fabric, place the center of modified template B over a corner point of any hexagon. Rotate the template until the dashed lines lie directly over the 3 converging seams. Trace around the template. Repeat the tracing process in each corner of each hexagon.

3. Cut out all of the triangles, and lay them on the work surface in exactly the same position they had before cutting.

4. Carefully rotate the 6 triangles that formed one of the original hexagons so that the 6 points that share the same fabric meet in the center. Repeat for the remaining triangles.

5. Separate the triangles into 4 diagonal rows as shown. Stitch the triangles in each row together. Press the seams of alternate rows in opposite directions. Then stitch the rows together, matching the seams at the center of each swirligig.

6. Refer to "Pressing Matters" on page 15 to press the stitched piece.

7. Trim ⅛" to ¼" from each side to straighten the edges.

Add the Borders

1. Stitch a border strip to one side of the stitched piece. Cut the ends even with the 2 adjacent sides.

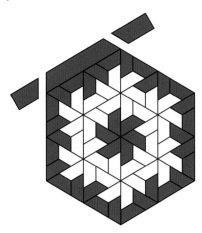

2. Working clockwise around the hexagon, add a border strip to each remaining side, cutting the strip even with the adjacent sides after each addition.

Finish the Quilt

Refer to "Finishing Techniques" on pages 64–67.

1. Center and layer the quilt top and batting over the backing; baste.
2. Quilt as desired.
3. Bind the quilt edges.

Swirligig Wreath Variation
Designed by Martha Thompson, 2001, Seattle, Washington, 26" x 23".
Pieced and quilted by Barbara Clouse.

Swirligig Wreath Variation

The body of this quilt is constructed in the same way as "Swirligig Wreath," but triangular pieces are used for the border rather than strips, and a third fabric is added for the binding.

Materials

All yardage is based on 42"-wide fabric unless otherwise stated.

1 yd. print for wreath and borders

⅞ yd. coordinating print for background

⅞ yd. fabric for backing

¼ yd. solid for binding

27" x 30" rectangle of batting

Template plastic

Cutting

From the binding fabric, cut:

> 2 strips, each 2½" x 42"

Instructions

1. Follow the instructions for "Swirligig Wreath" on pages 19–20 up to "Add the Borders."
2. Referring to "Making the Templates" on page 9, trace pattern C on page 70 onto template plastic. Mark the template and cut it out.
3. Using template C and referring to "Cutting Out the Hexagons" on page 10, cut 6 template C pieces from the remaining wreath fabric.
4. Stitch a template C piece to each side of the pieced hexagon.

5. Finish the quilt in the same manner as "Swirligig Wreath."

Free Floating
Designed by Martha Thompson, 2001, Seattle, Washington, 90" x 102".
Pieced by Margaret Schiebe; quilted by Sally Howard.

Free Floating

True to its name, the swirligigs float free and easy through this queen-size quilt. And because the placement for each one is random, you get to be the designer and decide where to put them! Using the design sheet on page 29 and a few scraps of your focal and background fabrics, arrange and rearrange to your heart's content. Then cut out the hexagons and start the tessellating process. It's that easy. Be sure to save the smaller hexagons that are left after cutting the triangles for use in another project.

Materials

All yardage is based on 42"-wide fabric unless otherwise stated.

9¾ yds. multicolor print for background, borders, and binding

⅞ yd. *each* of 13 assorted solids for swirligigs

8 yds. fabric for backing

King-size batting

Template plastic

Cutting

From the background fabric, cut:

    3 strips, each 14" x 94", on the lengthwise grain, for borders

    24 rectangles, each 3½" x 5", for background filler triangles. Cut 12 rectangles in half diagonally; cut the remaining 12 rectangles in half on the opposite diagonal.

    10 strips, each 2½" x 42", for binding

Design Your Quilt

1. Photocopy the design sheet on page 29.
2. Lay the template plastic over the design sheet. Using a permanent marker, trace around one of the whole hexagons. Cut out the template.
3. Using the template, trace a minimum of 8 hexagons onto each of the 13 assorted solids. Cut them out. Place the hexagons as desired on the unshaded hexagons on the design sheet. Leave empty spaces scattered throughout where the background fabric will be. You do not have to use all of the hexagons, and you may cut out more of any color you desire. Remember, you are the designer.
4. When you are satisfied with the arrangement, glue the fabric hexagons in place. Keep in mind that the remaining white spaces, as well as the

shaded spaces around the edges, will be cut from the background fabric. If you like, cut hexagons from the background fabric and glue them in place to make your design sheet more complete.

5. Count and make a note of the number of whole hexagons of background fabric needed (be sure to include the 8 whole hexagons in the shaded areas). Count and make a note of the number of whole hexagons of each of the swirligig fabrics needed.

Cut Out and Assemble the Hexagons

1. Referring to "Making the Templates" on page 9, trace pattern D on page 71 and pattern E on page 72 onto template plastic. Mark the templates and cut them out.

2. Using template D and referring to "Cutting Out the Hexagons" on page 10, cut out the required number of whole hexagons from the background and swirligig fabrics. Cut 7 additional whole hexagons from the background fabric; cut these 7 hexagons in half as shown.

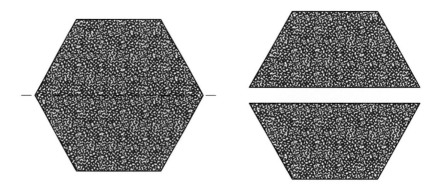

3. Modify template D by cutting across it on the modification line. Using the new template, trace 28 modified hexagons onto the wrong side of the remaining background fabric. Mark the corner dots, then cut out the modified hexagons.

4. Arrange the solid-color and background-print hexagons, the halved background hexagons, and the modified background hexagons as shown on your design sheet. Refer to "Piecing the Hexagons" on page 11 to stitch the hexagons together.

5. Refer to "Pressing Matters" on page 15 to press the stitched piece.

Cut Out the Triangles and Form the Swirligigs

1. Working on the right side of the stitched piece, place the center of template E over one corner of any hexagon. Rotate the template until the dashed lines lie directly over the 3 converging seams. Trace around the template. Repeat the tracing process in each corner of each whole hexagon.

2. Cut out 2 to 3 vertical rows of triangles at a time, and lay them on the work surface in exactly the same position they had before cutting.

3. Carefully rotate the 6 triangles that formed one of the original hexagons so that the 6 points that share the same fabric meet in the center. Repeat for the remaining triangles.

4. Separate the triangles into vertical rows as shown. Referring to "Cutting Out the Triangles and Forming the Swirligigs" on page 12, sew the triangles in each row together. Stitch a background filler triangle to the top and bottom of each row. Refer to "Pressing Matters" on page 15 to press the seam allowances.

5. Stitch the rows together as you complete them so you can see the pattern develop. When all of the rows have been stitched together, press the quilt top carefully, referring to "Pressing Matters" on page 15.

6. Referring to "Adding Borders" on page 64, stitch a border strip to each side of the quilt top. Stitch the remaining border strip to the bottom edge of the quilt top.

Finish the Quilt

Refer to "Finishing Techniques" on pages 64–67.

1. Center and layer the quilt top and batting over the backing; baste.
2. Quilt as desired.
3. Bind the quilt edges.
4. Add a hanging sleeve, if desired.

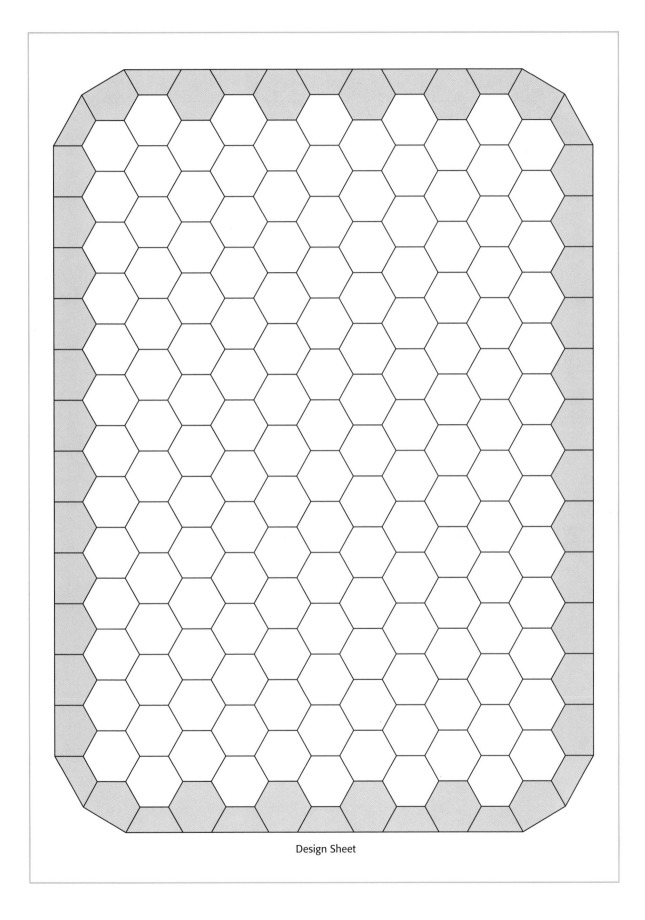

Design Sheet

Line Dance

By Martha Thompson, 2001, Seattle, Washington, 55½" x 64½".

Line Dance

I made this quilt with leftover hexagons from "Free Floating." Of course, I've given yardage instructions so you can start from scratch. If you decide to use leftover hexagons, you need make only the triangular part of the template.

Materials

All yardage is based on 42"-wide fabric unless otherwise stated.

¼ yd. *each* of 12 assorted solids for swirligigs

4½ yds. multicolor print for background and borders

1¾ yds. coordinating dark solid for alternating strips and binding

4 yds. fabric for backing

Twin-size batting

Template plastic

Cutting

From the background fabric, cut:

>   2 strips, each 6½" x 45", on the lengthwise grain, for top and bottom borders

>   2 strips, each 6½" x 68", on the lengthwise grain, for side borders

>   10 rectangles, each 2¼" x 4", for background filler triangles. Cut 5 rectangles in half diagonally; cut the remaining 5 rectangles in half on the opposite diagonal.

From the coordinating dark solid, cut:

>   4 strips, each 3½" x 54", on the lengthwise grain, for alternating strips

>   5 strips, each 2½" x 54", on the lengthwise grain, for binding

Cut Out and Assemble the Hexagons

1. Referring to "Making the Templates" on page 9, trace pattern F on page 73 onto template plastic. Mark the template and cut it out.

2. Using template F and referring to "Cutting Out the Hexagons" on page 10, cut a total of 70 hexagons from the 12 assorted solid fabrics. Cut 100 hexagons from the background fabric.

3. Referring to the illustrations at right, arrange the solid-color hexagons into 5 vertical rows of 14 hexagons each. Add a background hexagon to the beginning and end of each row. Arrange the background hexagons into 6 vertical rows of 15 hexagons each. Refer to "Piecing the Hexagons" on page 11 to stitch the hexagons into rows. Do not press yet.

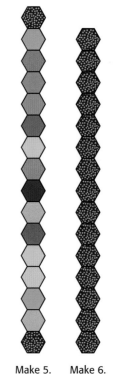

Make 5.   Make 6.

4. Beginning and ending with a background row, alternately stitch the 6 background and 5 solid-color hexagon rows together as shown at left.

5. Refer to "Pressing Matters" on page 15 to press the stitched piece.

Cut Out the Triangles and Form the Swirligigs

1. Modify template F by cutting along the inner solid lines, leaving the triangle that was inside the hexagon.

2. Working on the right side of the stitched piece, place the center of the triangle template over one corner of any hexagon. Rotate the template until the dashed lines lie directly over the 3 converging seams. Trace around the template. Repeat the tracing process in each corner of each solid-color hexagon.

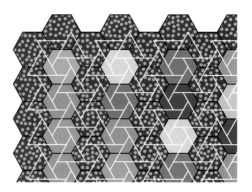

3. Cut out the triangles from the first 2 vertical rows of hexagons. Lay them on the work surface in exactly the same position they had before cutting.

4. Carefully rotate the 6 triangles that formed one of the original hexagons so that the 6 points that share the same fabric meet in the center. Repeat for the remaining triangles. A long line of 14 swirligigs will appear.

5. Separate the triangles into 2 vertical rows as shown at left. Stitch each row of triangles together, adding a background filler triangle to each end. Refer to "Pressing Matters" on page 15 to press the seams. Stitch the 2 rows together.

6. Working with 2 adjacent vertical rows at a time, repeat steps 3–5 above with the triangles in each of the remaining hexagon rows to make a total of 5 swirligig rows.

7. Refer to "Pressing Matters" on page 15 to press the seams in each row.

8. Alternating swirligig rows and dark solid strips, and beginning and ending with a swirligig row, stitch the 5 swirligig rows and the 4 dark solid strips together. Trim the solid strip ends even with the swirligig rows.

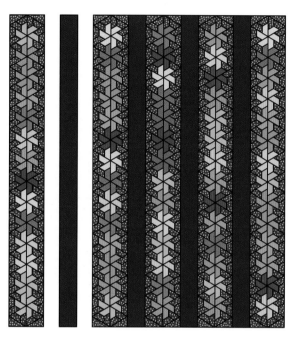

9. Refer to "Pressing Matters" on page 15 to press the stitched piece.

10. Refer to "Adding Borders" on page 64 to stitch the borders to the quilt top.

Finish the Quilt

Refer to "Finishing Techniques" on pages 64–67.

1. Center and layer the quilt top and batting over the backing; baste.

2. Quilt as desired.

3. Bind the quilt edges.

4. Add a hanging sleeve, if desired.

Epic Changes
By Martha Thompson, 2001, Seattle, Washington, 31½" x 53½".

Epic Changes

A collection of favorite fabrics finds expression in this contemporary wall hanging, a reflection on change. Use a few patchwork tricks to merge the energetic foreground into the slower-moving background. Choose your four background fabrics first, because the really important movement in this design is happening quietly there.

Materials

All yardage is based on 42"-wide fabric unless otherwise stated.

¼ yd. *each* of 6 or more assorted prints and solids for swirligigs

⅝ yd. *each* of 4 assorted background prints

1⅞ yds. fabric for backing

½ yd. print for binding

Crib-size batting

Template plastic

Cutting

From each of the 4 background fabrics, cut:

> 1 rectangle, 18½" x 32"

Design Your Quilt

1. Label the background prints 1–4.
2. Photocopy the design sheet on page 39.
3. Lay the template plastic over the design sheet. Using a permanent marker, trace around one of the whole hexagons. Cut out the template.
4. Using the template, cut 8 hexagons from each of background prints 2 and 3. Cut 2 hexagons from each of the prints in half as shown; discard one half from each fabric. Place the 6 half and 12 whole background hexagons where indicated in the shaded areas on the design sheet. Glue them in place.

5. Using the template, trace 4 hexagons onto each of the 6 assorted swirligig prints and solids. Cut them out. Arrange the hexagons as desired on the unshaded spaces on the design sheet. You do not have to use all of the hexagons, and you may cut out more of any color you desire.

6. When you are satisfied with the arrangement, glue the fabric hexagons in place.

Cut Out and Assemble the Hexagons

1. Referring to "Making the Templates" on page 9, trace pattern B on page 69 onto template plastic. Mark the template and cut it out.

2. Using template B and referring to "Cutting Out the Hexagons" on page 10, cut out the required number of whole hexagons from the swirligig fabrics. Cut 8 hexagons from each of the 2 background fabrics used for the shaded areas on the design sheet. Cut 2 of the hexagons from each of the 2 background fabrics in half; discard one half hexagon of each fabric.

3. Arrange the whole and half hexagons as on your design sheet. Refer to "Piecing the Hexagons" on page 11 to stitch the hexagons together.

4. Refer to "Pressing Matters" on page 15 to press the stitched piece.

5. Place a safety pin in the uppermost hexagon, or mark it in some other way, so that you can maintain the correct orientation of the pieces when they are incorporated into the background later.

Cut Out the Triangles and Form the Swirligigs

1. Modify template B by cutting along the inner solid lines, leaving the triangle that was inside the hexagon.

2. Working on the right side of the stitched piece, place the center of template B over a corner point of any hexagon. Rotate the template until the dashed lines lie directly over the 3 converging seams. Trace around the template. Repeat the tracing process in each corner of each hexagon.

3. Cut out all of the triangles and lay them on the work surface in exactly the same position they had before cutting.

4. Carefully rotate the 6 triangles that formed one of the original hexagons so that the 6 points that share the same fabric meet in the center. Repeat for the remaining triangles.

5. Separate the triangles into 6 vertical rows as shown. Stitch the triangles in each row together. Press the seams of alternate rows in opposite directions. Then stitch the rows together, matching the seams at the center of each swirligig.

6. Refer to "Pressing Matters" on page 15 to press the stitched piece.
7. Trim ⅛" to ¼" from each side to straighten the edges. Use template B to locate and mark the 6 corner dots on this large pieced hexagon. Mark the uppermost swirligig hexagon to indicate the top of the piece.

Set the Pieced Hexagon into the Background

1. Cut the 4 background rectangles in half diagonally from the bottom right corner to the top left corner. Arrange and sew together 6 of the triangles as shown to make 1 large rectangle. Press the seam allowances open.

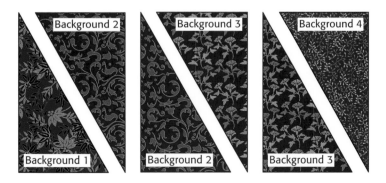

2. Lay the pieced background rectangle right side down on the work surface. Center the pieced hexagon right side down on top of the background rectangle. Make sure the uppermost swirligig hexagon is positioned at the top of the background rectangle.

3. Lightly trace the perimeter of the hexagon onto the background rectangle. Set aside the pieced hexagon. Use template B to locate and mark the 6 corner dots on the marked hexagon on the background rectangle.

4. Working on the wrong side of the background piece, measure ½" in from the 6 perimeter lines and mark the cutting line. Cut along the cutting line. Remove the large hexagon of background fabric. Clip into each corner up to the corner dot.

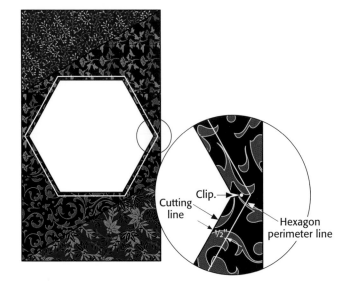

5. Position the pieced hexagon in the background opening. Check to be sure the uppermost swirligig is at the top of the rectangle. Pin the fabric edges, right sides together, aligning the corner dots. Stitch from one dot to the next dot, backstitching at each dot to reinforce the corner. Press the seams toward the background.

Finish the Quilt

Refer to "Finishing Techniques" on pages 64–67.

1. Center and layer the quilt top and batting over the backing; baste.

2. Quilt as desired.

3. Bind the quilt edges.

4. Add a hanging sleeve, if desired.

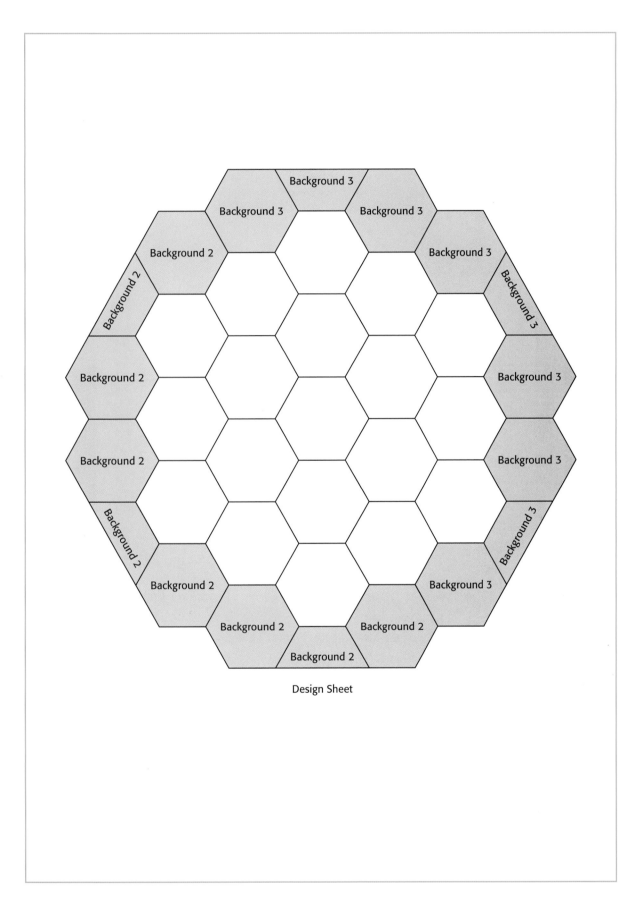

Design Sheet

Windmills of My Mind

Designed by Martha Thompson, 2001, Seattle, Washington, 40" x 56".

Pieced and quilted by Patty Federighi.

Windmills of My Mind

The shapes in this wall hanging were inspired by windmills I saw on a trip to the Netherlands—even though these shapes have six "blades" and interlock as none do there. The blades form swirligigs as in the other projects in this book, but here we arrive at the finished quilt by using simple patchwork triangles and traditional piecing techniques.

Materials

All yardage is based on 42"-wide fabric unless otherwise stated.

¼ yd. *each* of 12 assorted solids for swirligigs and inner border

1 yd. *each* of 2 prints for background and outer border

2⅞ yds. fabric for backing

½ yd. print for binding

Twin-size batting

Template plastic

Fabric gluestick

Cutting

From 4 of the 12 assorted solids, cut:

    1 strip, 1½" x 42", for inner borders

From each of the 2 background prints, cut:

    2 strips, each 2½" x 42", for outer borders

    3 strips, each 4¼" x 42", for background triangles

Cut Out the Triangles and Windmill Blades

1. Referring to "Making the Templates" on page 9, trace patterns G and H on page 74 onto template plastic. Mark the templates and cut them out.

2. Using template G, cut a total of 138 triangles from the six 4¼" x 42" background strips.

3. Fold each of the 12 swirligig fabrics in half, right sides together and with selvages aligned. Using template H, trace 6 blades onto each of the 12 fabrics. Place a pin in the center of each blade to keep the 2 layers together. Cut out the blades. Do not remove the pins.

Assemble the Triangles and Windmill Blades

1. Using a ¼" seam allowance, stitch along the curved edges of each blade. Leave the long, straight edge open. Clip the curved edges. Turn each blade to the right side. Gently push out the point at the top of each blade; press.

2. Working on a large, flat surface, arrange the triangles as shown. Position the blades over the triangles where indicated, or arrange them as you wish. Be sure to align the straight edge of each blade with the edge of the triangle. When you are satisfied with the arrangement, apply a small amount of glue to the underside of each blade where indicated on the template, and press them into place on the triangles. Avoid placing glue in the seam allowances.

3. Separate the triangles into diagonal rows. Stitch the triangles in each row together. Refer to "Pressing Matters" on page 15 to press the seams. Stitch the rows together. Press the stitched piece.

4. Cut a large triangle from the remainder of each of the 2 background fabrics to fill in the upper left and lower right corners. To do this, lay the background fabrics under the stitched piece, shifting them until they fill the appropriate spaces. Draw a line on each of the background fabrics along the edges of the stitched piece. Remove the stitched piece. Using a long ruler, cut ½" beyond the marked lines in the background fabrics.

5. Sew the background triangles to the stitched piece, using a ¼" seam allowance.

6. Trim the edges of the stitched piece as shown.

Trim here.

Trim here.

Add the Borders

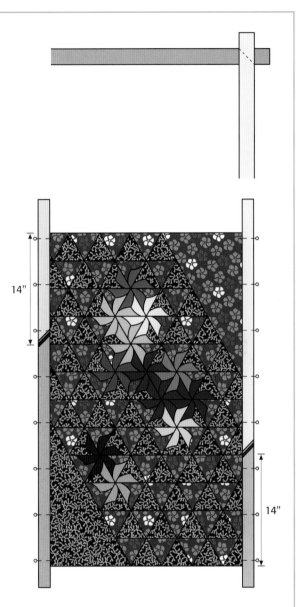

1. To make the pieced inner border, stitch the ends of 2 of the inner border strips together on the diagonal as shown at right. Trim the seam allowance to ¼"; press the seam allowance open. Repeat for the remaining 2 inner border strips.

2. With right sides together and raw edges matching, pin the pieced border strips to the sides of the quilt top, positioning the seams as shown at right. Stitch the strips to the quilt sides. Trim the ends even with the top and bottom edges of the quilt, saving the trimmed strips to use in step 3. Press the seam allowances toward the borders.

3. Stitch the 2 strips from the top of the quilt together on the diagonal. Repeat for the 2 strips from the bottom of the quilt.

4. With right sides together and raw edges matching, position the strips on the quilt top and bottom edges so they meet the border strips of the same color on the quilt sides. Stitch the strips to the quilt top and bottom edges. Press the seam allowances toward the borders.

5. Refer to "Adding Borders" on page 64 to stitch the outer border strips to the quilt top, piecing the strips together as needed.

Finish the Quilt

Refer to "Finishing Techniques" on pages 64–67.

1. Center and layer the quilt top and batting over the backing; baste.

2. Quilt as desired.

3. Bind the quilt edges.

4. Add a hanging sleeve, if desired.

Hexagon with the Wind
By Martha Thompson, 2001, Seattle, Washington, 40" x 51".

Hexagon with the Wind

The hexagons left over from "Windmills of My Mind" (page 40) are perfect for piecing this beauty. Just randomly sprinkle the brightest ones over a field of neutral background fabrics to achieve the spontaneity of windblown leaves.

Materials

All yardage is based on 42"-wide fabric unless otherwise stated.

¼ yd. *each* of 10 assorted solids for swirligigs and binding

½ yd. *each* of 8 or more neutral prints and solids close in color and value, for background

2⅝ yds. fabric for backing

Twin-size batting

Template plastic

Design Your Quilt

1. Photocopy the design sheet on page 48.
2. Lay the template plastic over the design sheet. Using a permanent marker, trace around one of the hexagons. Cut out the template.
3. Using the template, trace 3 or 4 hexagons onto the wrong side of each of the swirligig fabrics. If you are using leftover hexagons from "Windmills of My Mind," trace the hexagons onto leftover scraps of those hexagon fabrics. Cut out the hexagons. Place them as desired on the unshaded hexagons on the design sheet. Try to arrange the hexagons to represent windblown leaves. You do not have to use all of the hexagons, and you may cut out more of any color you desire.
4. When you are satisfied with the arrangement, glue the fabric hexagons in place. The remaining white spaces, as well as the shaded spaces around the edges, will be cut from the background fabrics. If you like, cut hexagons from the background fabrics, arrange them randomly, and glue them in place to make the design sheet complete.

Cut Out and Assemble the Hexagons

1. Referring to "Making the Templates" on page 9, trace pattern I on page 75 and pattern J on page 76 onto template plastic. Mark the templates and cut them out.

2. Using template I and referring to "Cutting Out the Hexagons" on page 10, cut out the required number of whole hexagons from each of the 10 swirligig fabrics and the 8 background fabrics.

3. Arrange the swirligig and background hexagons as shown on your design sheet. Refer to "Piecing the Hexagons" on page 11 to stitch the hexagons together.

4. Refer to "Pressing Matters" on page 15 to press the stitched piece.

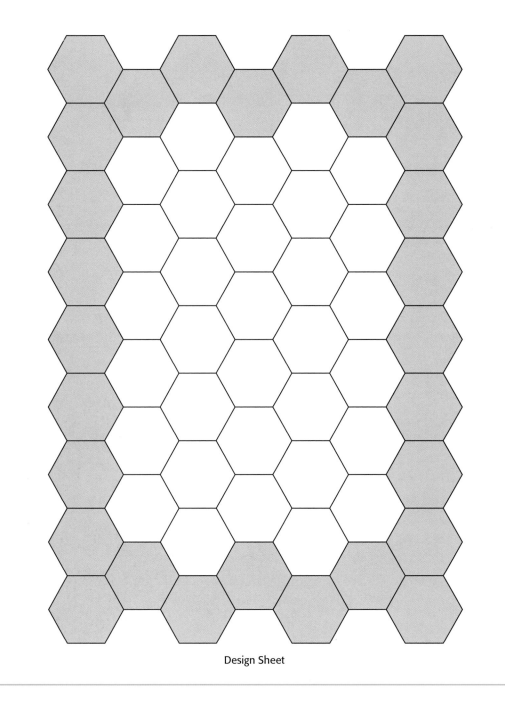

Design Sheet

Cut Out the Triangles and Form the Swirligigs

1. Working on the right side of the stitched piece, place the center of template J over the corner of any hexagon where 3 seams meet. Rotate the template until the dashed lines lie directly over the 3 converging seams. Trace around the template. Repeat the tracing process in each corner of each hexagon where 3 seams meet. You will not be able to trace triangles on the outermost edges of the stitched piece.

2. Cut out all of the triangles, and lay them on the work surface in exactly the same position they had before cutting.

3. Carefully rotate the 6 triangles that formed one of the original hexagons so that the 6 points that share the same fabric meet in the center. Repeat for the remaining triangles, matching all 6 points of each swirligig (partial swirligigs will be created along the outer edges).

4. Separate the triangles into diagonal rows as shown at right. Stitch the triangles in each row together. Refer to "Pressing Matters" on page 15 to press the seams. Stitch the rows together, matching the seams at the center of each swirligig.

5. Refer to "Pressing Matters" on page 15 to press the stitched piece.

Finish the Quilt

Refer to "Finishing Techniques" on pages 64–67.

1. Center and layer the quilt top and batting over the backing; baste.

2. Quilt as desired.

3. To bind the quilt with a pieced binding, cut a 2½"-wide strip from the remainder of each of the swirligig fabrics. Stitch the strips together into one long strip approximately 170" long. Bind the quilt edges.

4. Add a hanging sleeve, if desired.

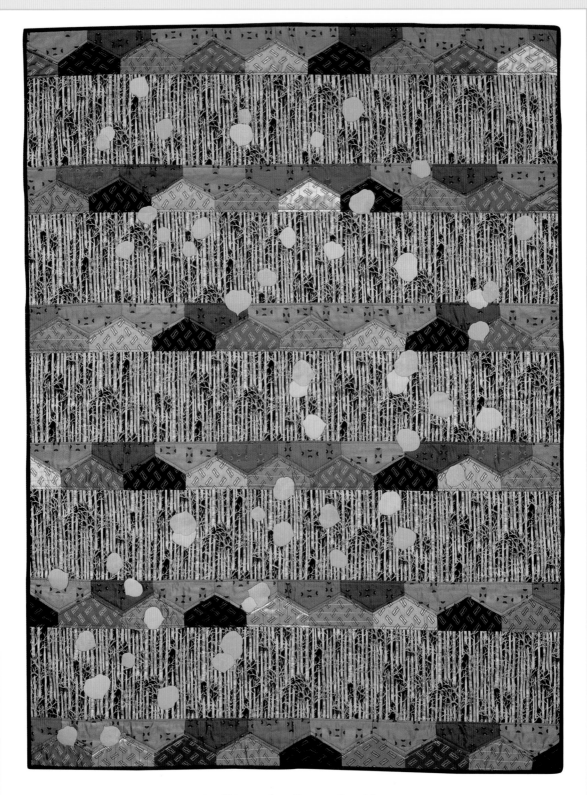

A Simple Bar Quilt
By Martha Thompson, 2001, Seattle, Washington, 52" x 75".

A Simple Bar Quilt

My collection of beautiful Italian silks inspired this easy-to-make quilt. The weight of the silk blended well with that of the cotton print. I minimized the problem of stretching by carefully orienting the straight grain of each hexagon horizontally. Just sew the hexagons together into rows, then slice the rows in half. Alternate the hexagon rows with a wide strip of an interesting print, then fuse the free-floating leaf shapes in place as desired. Or, instead of leaves, choose a motif from your printed fabric or pluck a shape from your imagination to sprinkle freely over your quilt.

Materials

All yardage is based on 42"-wide fabric unless otherwise stated.

¼ yd. *each* of 11 assorted prints for hexagon bars

2 yds. large-scale print for alternating bars

⅛ yd. *each* of 3 or more bright solids for appliqués

½ yd. coordinating solid for binding

Twin-size batting

½ yd. paper-backed fusible web

Template plastic

Cutting

From the large-scale print, cut:

    7 strips, each 9½" x 42", for alternating bars

From the coordinating solid, cut:

    7 strips, each 2½" x 42", for binding

Cut Out and Assemble the Hexagons

1. Referring to "Making the Templates" on page 9, trace the hexagon portion of pattern B on page 69 onto template plastic. Mark the template and cut it out.

2. Using template B and referring to "Cutting Out the Hexagons" on page 10, cut a total of 54 hexagons from the hexagon-bar fabrics.

3. Stitch the hexagons into 6 horizontal rows of 9 hexagons each, having the grain line of each hexagon running horizontally. The edges will be slightly bias, so handle them carefully. Stitch the rows together.

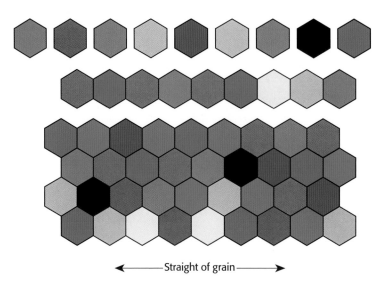

Straight of grain

4. Refer to "Pressing Matters" on page 15 to press the stitched piece.
5. Trim away half-hexagons on the left and right sides to make the edges even.

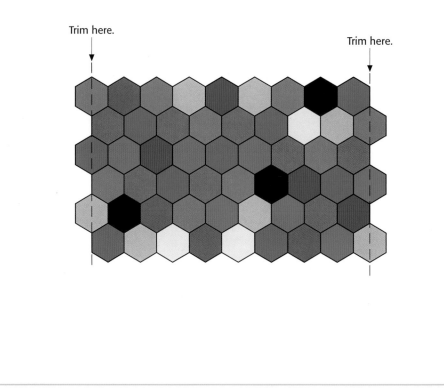

Trim here.   Trim here.

6. Cut through the center of each row of hexagons. This will create 5 complete bars, with 2 half bars from the top and bottom left over. To make a sixth complete bar, sew the uncut edges of the 2 half bars together in the same manner as in step 3 above. Refer to "Pressing Matters" on page 15 to press the seam allowances.

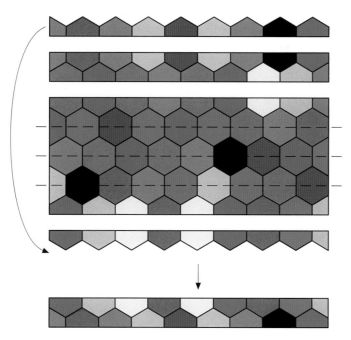

Assemble the Quilt

1. Stitch the large-scale print alternating bars together end to end to make one long strip. Press the seam allowances in one direction, or open, as you prefer. From the strip, cut 5 bars, each 9½" x 52".

2. Alternating a hexagon bar with a print bar, and beginning and ending with a hexagon bar, stitch the bars together horizontally. Press the seam allowances toward the print bars.

3. Think of a motif that expresses the theme of your quilt. It could be a flower, a leaf, or free form. Draw it in 3 sizes on paper. These are your 3 appliqué patterns. (Three sizes of leaves are given on page 54 for you to use if you desire.) Trace your patterns as many times as you like onto the paper side of the fusible web. Cut around the traced designs, leaving a ¼" margin. Follow the manufacturer's instructions to fuse the traced designs to the wrong side of the desired bright solid appliqué fabrics.

4. Cut out the appliqués on the traced lines, and remove the paper backing.

5. Position the appliqués on the quilt top as desired. Follow the manufacturer's instructions to fuse the appliqués to the quilt top. Add a bit of embroidery or other embellishment, or just leave them plain.

Finish the Quilt

Refer to "Finishing Techniques" on pages 64–67.

1. Center and layer the quilt top and batting over the backing; baste.
2. Quilt as desired.
3. Bind the quilt edges.
4. Add a hanging sleeve, if desired.

Appliqué Patterns

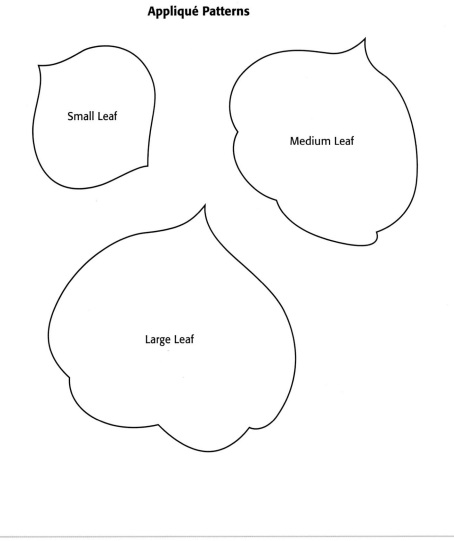

Small Leaf

Medium Leaf

Large Leaf

Double Dutch Treat
By Martha Thompson, 2001, Seattle, Washington, 26" x 35".

Double Dutch Treat

The traditional Thousand Pyramids design forms a backdrop that actually merges with the spinning, tessellated shapes in the foreground. It all happens automatically in the piecing process of this wall hanging–size quilt. Because the process is rather complex and different from that of the other quilts in this book, beginners may want to start with one of the easier projects before trying this one.

If you began with "Windmills of My Mind," your large hexagons are already cut and ready to use. Who knows what will happen to the trimmings from this quilt!

Materials

All yardage is based on 42"-wide fabric unless otherwise stated.

¼ yd. *each* of 6 to 9 assorted fabrics for swirligigs

1 yd. *each* of 1 light and 1 dark print for background and binding

1 yd. fabric for backing

Crib-size batting

Template plastic

Design Your Quilt

1. Photocopy the design sheet on page 59.
2. Lay the template plastic over the design sheet. Using a permanent marker, trace around one of the hexagons. Cut out the template.
3. Using the template, trace 1 hexagon onto each of the 6 to 9 swirligig fabrics. Cut them out. Place the hexagons as desired over the spaces on the design sheet. They will look best if butted against each other, but they do not all have to connect. Cut more hexagons if you like.
4. When you are satisfied with the arrangement, glue the fabric hexagons in place.
5. Decide which of the background fabrics you wish to use in the shaded background triangles on the design sheet, and which in the unshaded. Mark each fabric to indicate its placement.

Cut Out the Pieces

1. Referring to "Making the Templates" on page 9, trace patterns I, J, K, and L on pages 75–77 onto template plastic. Mark the templates and cut them out.

2. Using template I and referring to "Cutting Out the Hexagons" on page 10 and your design sheet, cut out the required number of hexagons from the swirligig fabrics.

3. Referring to the design sheet, count the number needed of each of the following: shaded triangles, unshaded triangles, shaded full caps, unshaded full caps, shaded half caps, and unshaded half caps. Note these numbers in the margin of the design sheet.

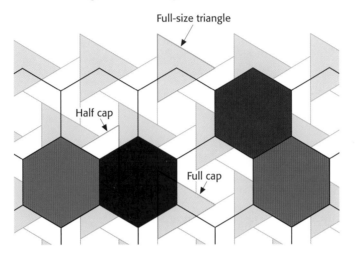

4. Using template J, cut the required number of shaded and unshaded triangles from the appropriate fabrics.

5. Using template K, cut the required number of shaded and unshaded full caps from the appropriate fabrics. Mark the pivot point on each full-cap piece, then cut out the pieces. Clip to each pivot point.

6. Using template L, cut the required number of shaded and unshaded half caps from the appropriate fabrics. Mark the corner dot on each half-cap piece, then cut them out.

Assemble the Pieces

1. Refer to your design sheet to lay out the hexagon pieces. Refer to "Piecing the Hexagons" on page 11 to stitch together the hexagons that are adjacent to each other.

2. Position the full-cap and half-cap pieces next to the hexagons as indicated on the design sheet. Overlap them just enough to be able to pin them temporarily in place. Stitch the full-cap and half-cap pieces in place, first by stitching a seam to the pivot point and backstitching. Then pivot the 2 fabric pieces, and align the 2 remaining edges. Stitch the second seam, backstitching at the pivot point. **Note:** The caps are all sewn to hexagons, not to other caps.

3. Refer to "Pressing Matters" on page 15 to press the stitched pieces.

4. Working on the right side of the stitched piece, place the center of the template J triangle over the corner of any hexagon where 3 seams meet. Rotate the template until the dashed lines lie directly over the 3 converging seams. Trace around the template. Repeat the tracing process in each corner of each hexagon where 3 seams meet.

5. Cut out all of the triangles, and lay them on the work surface in exactly the same position they had before cutting.

6. Carefully rotate the 6 triangles that formed one of the original hexagons so that the 6 points that share the same fabric meet in the center. Repeat for the remaining triangles.

7. Fill in the rest of the design with the remaining full-size background triangles, making sure that you alternate the 2 background fabrics. Use as many as needed to enlarge the patchwork to the size and shape you wish. If desired, fill large areas with large pieces of the leftover background fabrics instead of with cut triangles. (If you are using large pieces of background fabric to fill in the corners, stitch these to the quilt top after all the triangles have been stitched together. Square up the quilt edges as needed.)

8. Separate the triangles into diagonal rows as shown. Stitch the triangles in each row together. Refer to "Pressing Matters" on page 15 to press the seams. Stitch the rows together, matching the seams at the center of each swirligig.

9. Refer to "Pressing Matters" on page 15 to press the stitched piece.

Finish the Quilt

Refer to "Finishing Techniques" on pages 64–67.

1.   Center and layer the quilt top and batting over the backing; baste.

2.   Quilt as desired.

3.   Bind the quilt edges.

4.   Add a hanging sleeve, if desired.

Design Sheet

Poinsettias
By Martha Thompson, 2001, Seattle, Washington, 66" diameter.

Poinsettias

This round table topper looks lovely when draped over a larger linen or lace tablecloth. Or you could slit from one edge to the center, bind the edges, and use it as a Christmas-tree skirt. With large hexagons and easy piecing, this one goes together quickly so you can enjoy the holidays.

Materials

All yardage is based on 42"-wide fabric unless otherwise stated.

2 yds. red solid or print for poinsettia petals

3⅛ yds. green print for background

1¼ yds. coordinating stripe for center wreath hexagons and binding

4½ yds. fabric for backing

Twin-size batting

Template plastic

Fabric gluestick

90 brass beads, ¼" to ⁵⁄₁₆" diameter

Cut Out the Binding, Background, and Wreath Pieces

1. Fold the stripe fabric in half diagonally, right sides together. Cut along the fold. With the fabric still layered right sides together, make two 4"-wide cuts along the edge to make 4 bias strips. Set these aside for the binding.

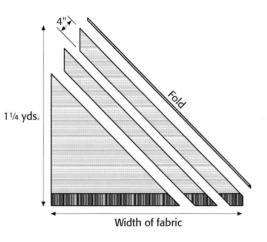

2. Referring to "Making the Templates" on page 9, trace patterns M, N, and O on pages 78–79 onto template plastic. Mark the templates and cut them out.

3. Using template M, cut 6 hexagons from the remaining stripe fabric and 22 hexagons from the green background fabric. Cut 9 of the background hexagons in half as shown.

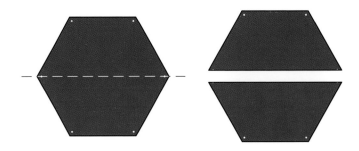

4. Using template N, cut 108 triangles from the remaining green background fabric.

Cut Out and Assemble the Poinsettia Petals

1. Fold the red fabric in half, right sides together with selvages aligned. Using template O, trace 108 poinsettia petals onto the wrong side of the fabric. Place a pin in the center of each petal to keep the 2 layers together. Cut out the petals. Do not remove the pins.

2. Using a ¼" seam allowance, stitch along the curved edges of each petal. Leave the long, straight edge open. Clip the curved edges. Turn each petal to the right side. Gently push out the point at the top of each petal; press.

Assemble the Poinsettia Hexagons

1. Arrange 6 background triangles into a hexagon. Position a petal over each triangle, with the straight edge of the petal aligned with the edge of the triangle, and the wide end of each petal toward the outer edge of the hexagon, as shown at right. When the petals have been positioned correctly, apply a small amount of glue to the underside of each petal where indicated on the template, and press them into place on the triangles. Avoid placing glue in the seam allowances.

2. Stitch the triangles together as shown at right to make a poinsettia hexagon. Make 18.

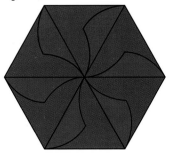

Assemble the Quilt

1. Refer to "Piecing the Hexagons" on page 11 to stitch 2 wreath hexagons, 4 full-size background hexagons, 6 poinsettia hexagons, and 6 half hexagons together as shown. Make 3 units.

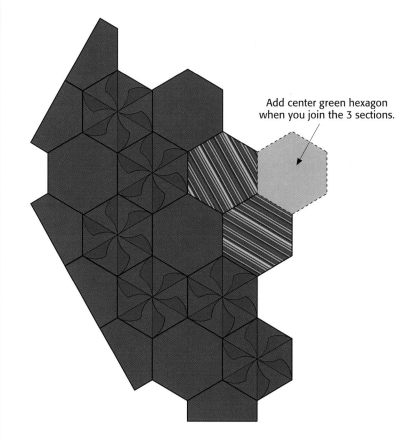

Add center green hexagon when you join the 3 sections.

2. Place the 3 units together so they interlock and make a circle. Stitch the units together, adding the center background hexagon to the units as you go.
3. Refer to "Pressing Matters" on page 15 to press the stitched piece.
4. Trim the quilt edge so it measures 66" in diameter.

Finish the Quilt

Refer to "Finishing Techniques" on pages 64–67.

1. Center and layer the quilt top and batting over the backing; baste.
2. Quilt as desired.
3. Stitch 5 brass beads to the center of each poinsettia hexagon.
4. Bind the quilt edges with the bias strips.

Finishing Techniques

Adding Borders

To border or not to border? This is a question that plagues many quilters when they have completed a quilt top. Borders aren't always necessary, as you can see by some of the projects in this book, but many times they are. For some quilts, borders are needed for aesthetic purposes; they serve as a visual frame for the composition, like the frame around a painting. For other quilts, they serve a practical purpose, such as to extend the size of the quilt to the necessary dimensions or to help "square it up." Most important, though, borders give us our last and best opportunity to stabilize the edges of the quilt. In quilts such as many of the ones presented in this book, where everything is slightly off grain, a sturdy border is necessary to stabilize the fabrics against stretching. Small quilts are not as likely to stretch out of shape as large quilts because they do not weigh as much, so binding alone can stabilize the edges. For large quilts with borders, I recommend cutting the border strips on the lengthwise fabric grain to eliminate any stretch factor (refer to "Fabric" on page 8).

Follow these directions to add borders to your quilt.

1. Measure the width of the quilt top through the horizontal center. Cut the top and bottom border strips to that measurement. Mark the centers of the border strips and the quilt top and bottom edges. Pin the borders to the top and bottom edges of the quilt top, right sides together, matching the center points and ends. Sew the border strips in place, using a ¼" seam allowance and easing (never stretching) as necessary. Press the seam allowances toward the border strips.

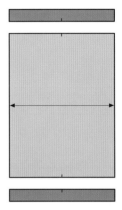

2. Measure the length of the quilt top through the vertical center, including the top and bottom borders you just added. Cut the side border strips to that measurement, piecing as necessary. Mark the centers of the border strips and the quilt sides. Pin the borders to the sides of the quilt top, right sides together, matching the center points and ends. Sew the border strips in place, using a ¼" seam allowance and easing as necessary. Press the seam allowances toward the border strips.

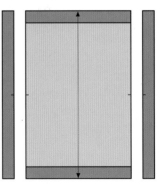

Layering and Basting

Once your quilt top is finished, you will need to layer it with batting and backing before you quilt it.

1. Mark the quilt top with the desired quilting design.

2. Cut the backing and batting approximately 4" larger than the pieced top. This will give you 2" extra on each side for the take-up that occurs during quilting. If it is necessary to piece the backing to get the necessary size, join 2 or 3 lengths of fabric as shown and press the seams open.

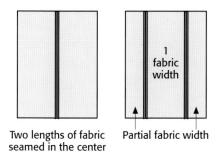

Two lengths of fabric   Partial fabric width
seamed in the center

3. Spread the backing, wrong side up, on a flat, clean surface. Anchor it with pins or masking tape. Be careful not to stretch the backing out of shape.

4. Spread the batting over the backing, smoothing out any wrinkles. I suggest using a thin polyester or cotton batting for quilts with interesting geometric shapes such as the ones in this book. With puffier battings, the points get lost in the thickness, and interesting quilting lines don't show up very well.

5. Spread out the pressed quilt top, right side up, on the batting. Smooth out any wrinkles and make sure the edges of the quilt top are parallel to the edges of the backing.

6. If you are hand quilting, hand baste the layers together with needle and thread, starting in the center and working outward. Baste in a grid of horizontal and vertical lines 6" to 8" apart. Finish by basting around the edges. If you are machine quilting, baste the layers together with #2 rustproof safety pins. Place pins 6" to 8" apart, away from the area you intend to quilt.

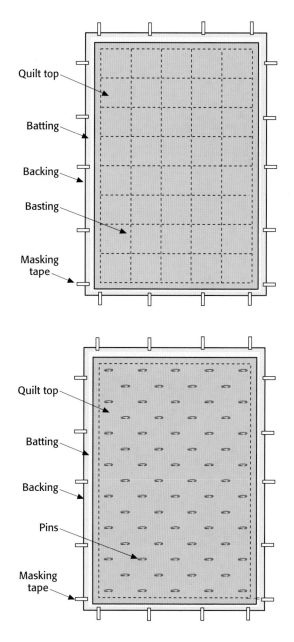

Quilting

The designs in this book are suitable for either hand or machine quilting. I prefer machine quilting at this busy time in my life, but please feel free to choose whichever method you are more comfortable with. When the quilting is complete, remove the thread basting or safety pins.

Binding

Once your quilt is quilted, it's time to finish the raw outer edges with binding.

1. Trim the batting and backing even with the quilt-top edges.
2. Cut 2½"-wide strips across the width of the fabric, unless otherwise indicated. Cut enough strips to go around the perimeter of the quilt, plus an additional 10" for seams and mitered corners.
3. Join the binding strips end to end with diagonal seams to make one long, continuous binding strip. Trim the excess fabric, leaving a ¼" seam allowance, and press the seam open.

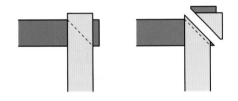

4. Cut one end of the binding strip at a 45° angle. Press the cut edge under ¼". Then press the binding strip in half lengthwise, wrong sides and raw edges together.

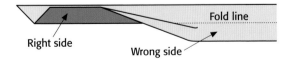

Right side   Fold line   Wrong side

5. Beginning with the angled end, place the binding strip along one edge of the quilt top several inches from a corner. Align the binding raw edges with the quilt raw edge. Leaving the first 6" of the binding unstitched, stitch the binding to the quilt top, using a ¼" seam allowance. End the stitching ¼" from the corner of the quilt; backstitch. Remove the quilt from the machine.

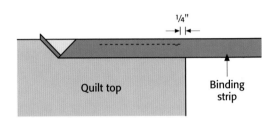

¼"

Quilt top   Binding strip

6. Turn the project so you are ready to sew the next side. Fold the binding straight up, creating a 45°-angle fold. Then fold the binding back down so the new fold is even with the top edge of the quilt and the binding raw edge is aligned with the side of the quilt. Beginning at the edge, stitch the binding to the quilt, stopping ¼" from the next corner. Repeat the folding and stitching process for each corner.

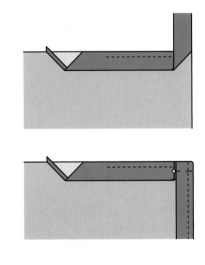

7. When you are approximately 6" from where you began stitching, overlap the end of the binding with the beginning of the binding about 1" and cut away the excess. Open up the binding end, and trim it at a 45° angle. Refold the binding, tuck the end into the beginning, and finish stitching the binding to the edge.

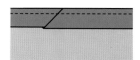

8. Fold the binding over the raw edge to the back of the quilt. Blindstitch it in place so the folded edge covers the row of machine stitching. A miter will form at each corner. Blindstitch the mitered corners in place.

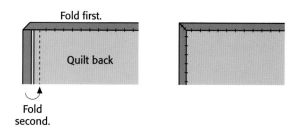

Fold first.

Quilt back

Fold second.

Adding a Hanging Sleeve

These quilts are meant to be displayed where everyone can view your workmanship. A hanging sleeve attached to the back of your quilt will aid you in hanging the quilt from a rod or dowel inserted though it and placed into carriers attached to your wall.

Follow these steps to make a hanging sleeve:

1. Measure the width of your quilt at the top. Cut a strip of fabric 5" to 9" wide and 1" less than the width measured. If needed, cut more than one strip and sew the ends together to create the desired length.

2. Press under each end ¼"; stitch close to the raw edge.

3. Fold the sleeve in half lengthwise, right sides together. Stitch the raw edges together. Turn the sleeve right side out; press.

4. Pin-mark the center point of the top edge of the quilt and the center point of the sleeve. Pin the folded edge of the sleeve next to the binding at the top edge of the quilt, aligning the center points. Blindstitch the folded edge in place.

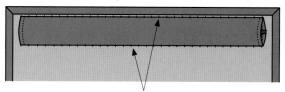

Blindstitch top and bottom of sleeve to quilt.

5. Blindstitch the bottom edge of the sleeve in place, pushing the sleeve up slightly and stitching just under the seam line. This will provide a little give so the hanging rod doesn't put strain on the quilt. Be careful not to catch the front of the quilt as you stitch.

Patterns

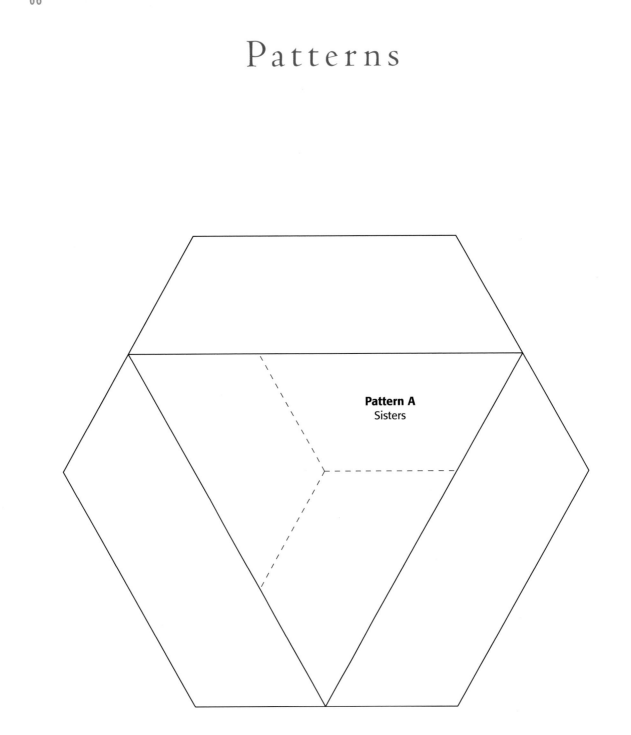

Pattern A
Sisters

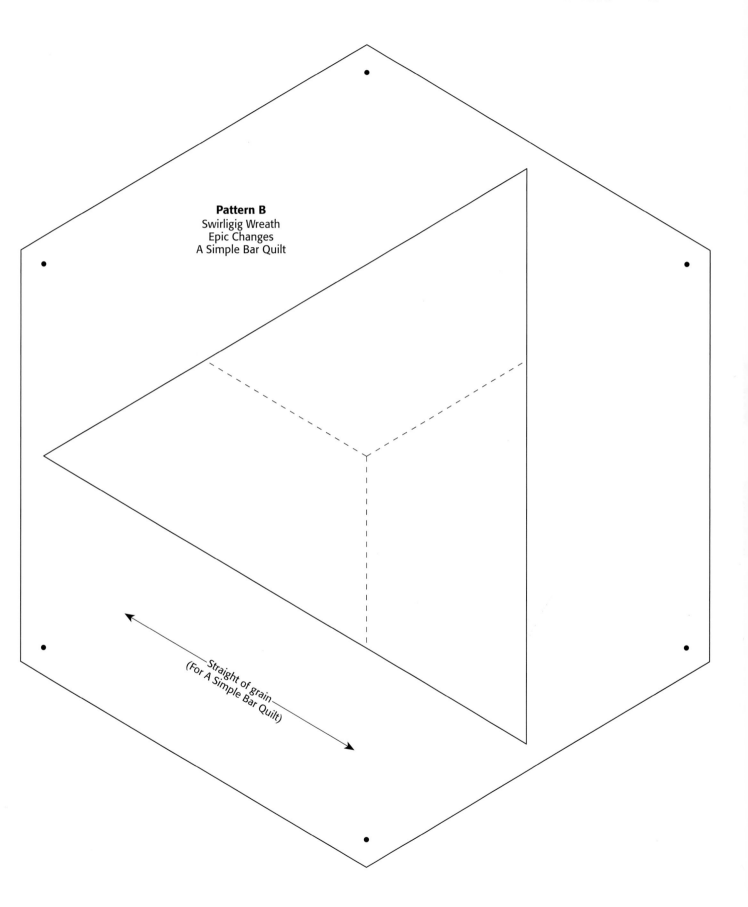

Pattern B
Swirligig Wreath
Epic Changes
A Simple Bar Quilt

Straight of grain
(For A Simple Bar Quilt)

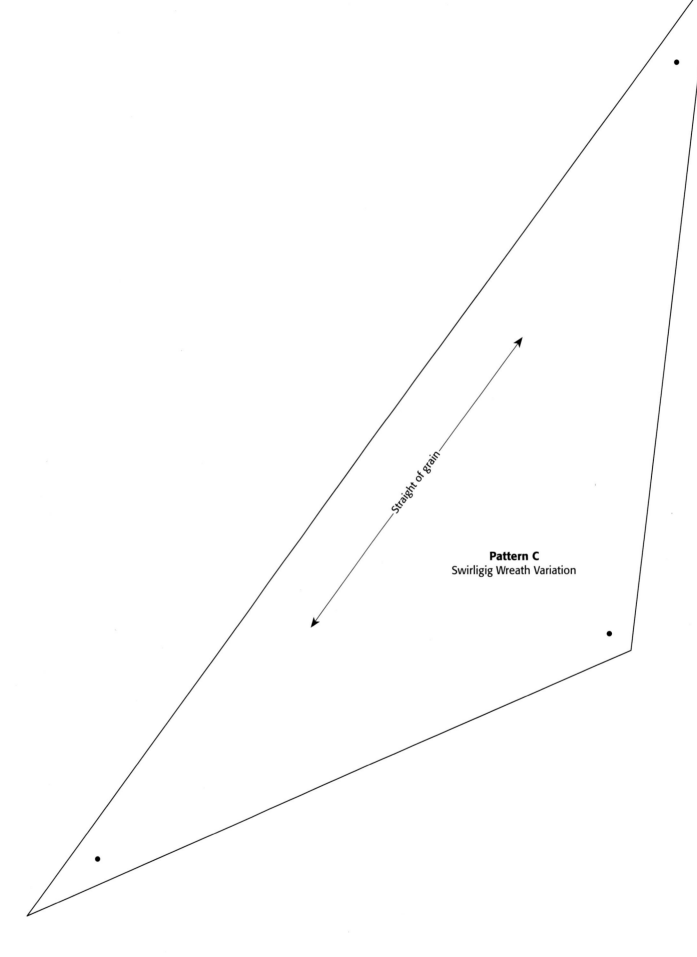

Straight of grain

Pattern C
Swirligig Wreath Variation

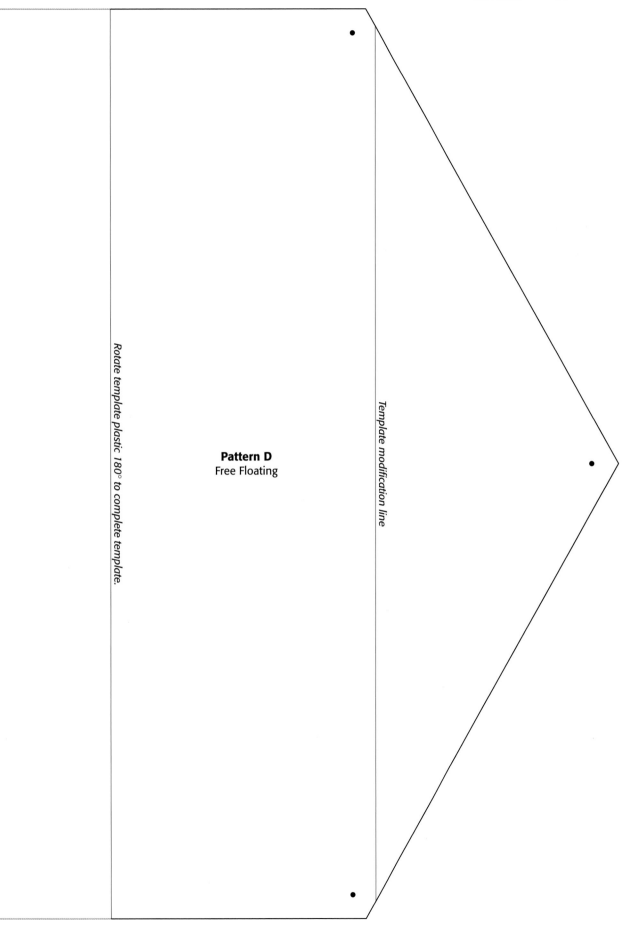

Rotate template plastic 180° to complete template.

Pattern D
Free Floating

Template modification line

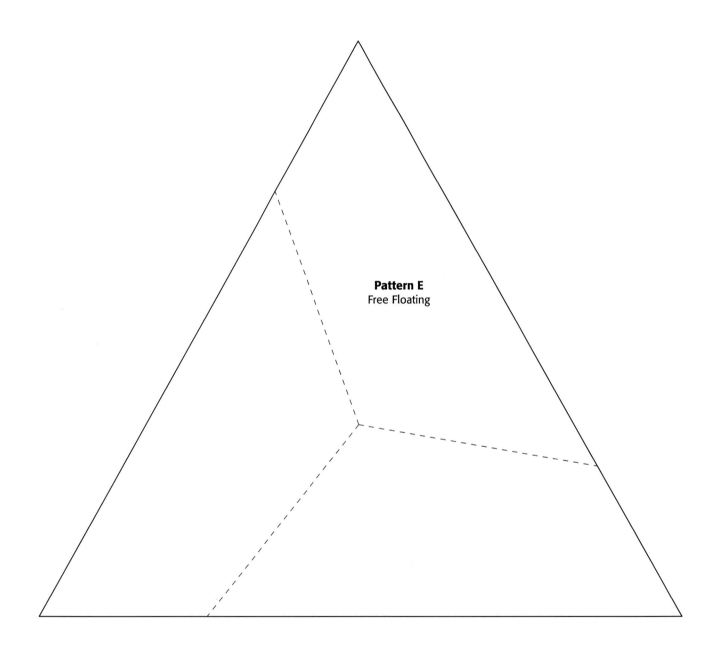

Pattern E
Free Floating

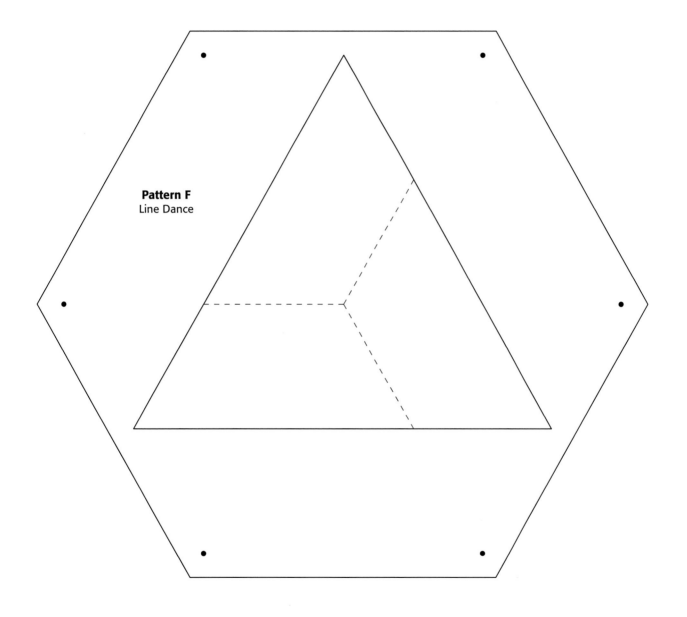

Pattern F
Line Dance

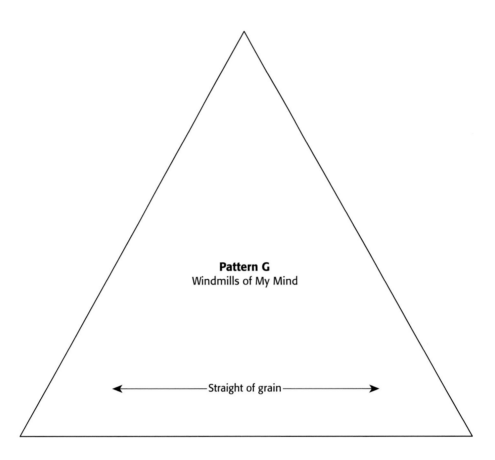

Pattern G
Windmills of My Mind

←————— Straight of grain —————→

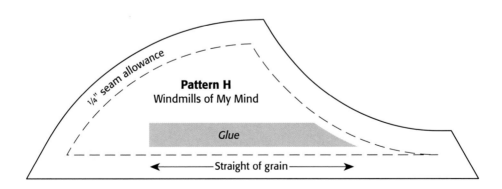

¼" seam allowance

Pattern H
Windmills of My Mind

Glue

←————— Straight of grain —————→

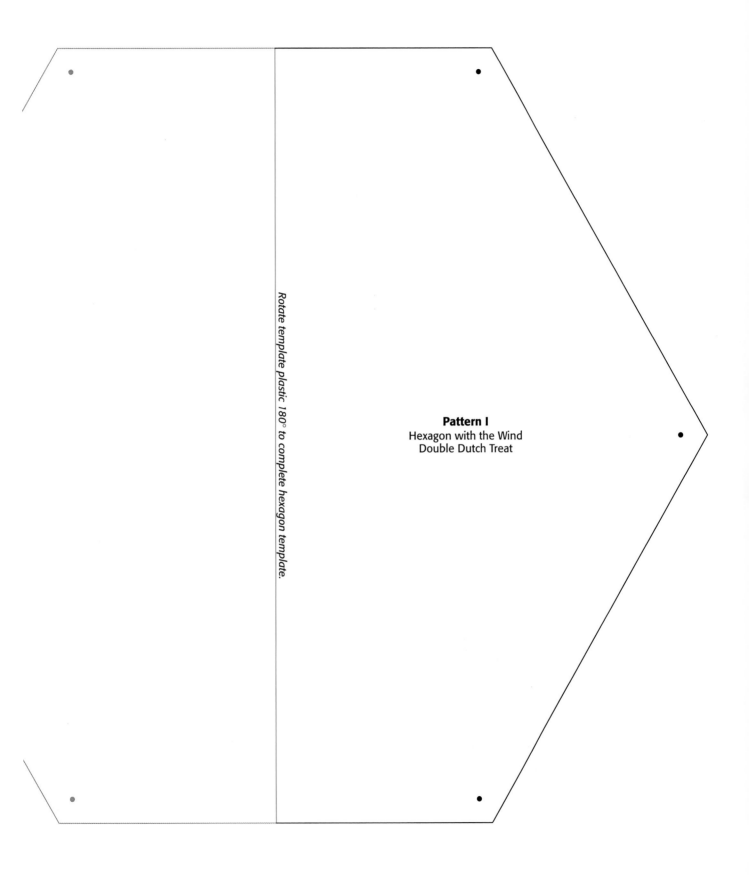

Rotate template plastic 180° to complete hexagon template.

Pattern I
Hexagon with the Wind
Double Dutch Treat

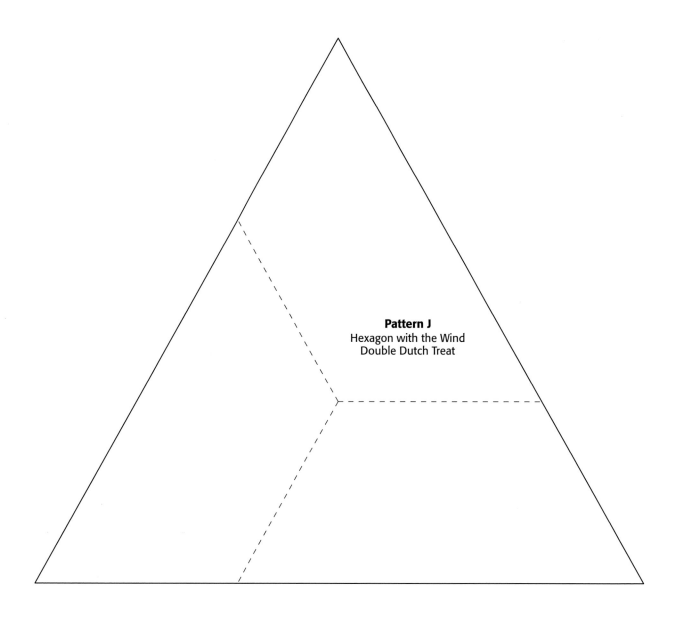

Pattern J
Hexagon with the Wind
Double Dutch Treat

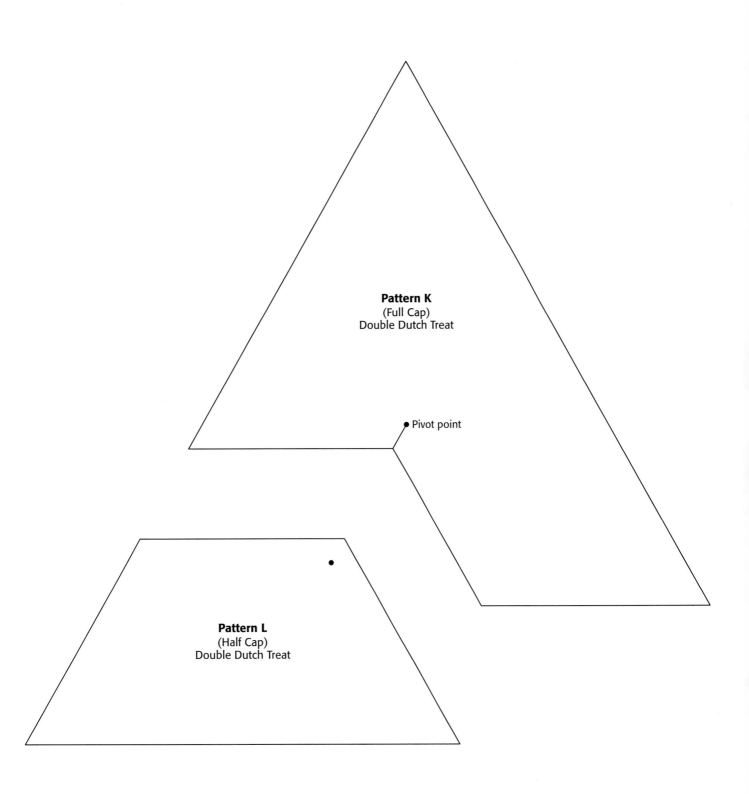

Pattern K
(Full Cap)
Double Dutch Treat

● Pivot point

Pattern L
(Half Cap)
Double Dutch Treat

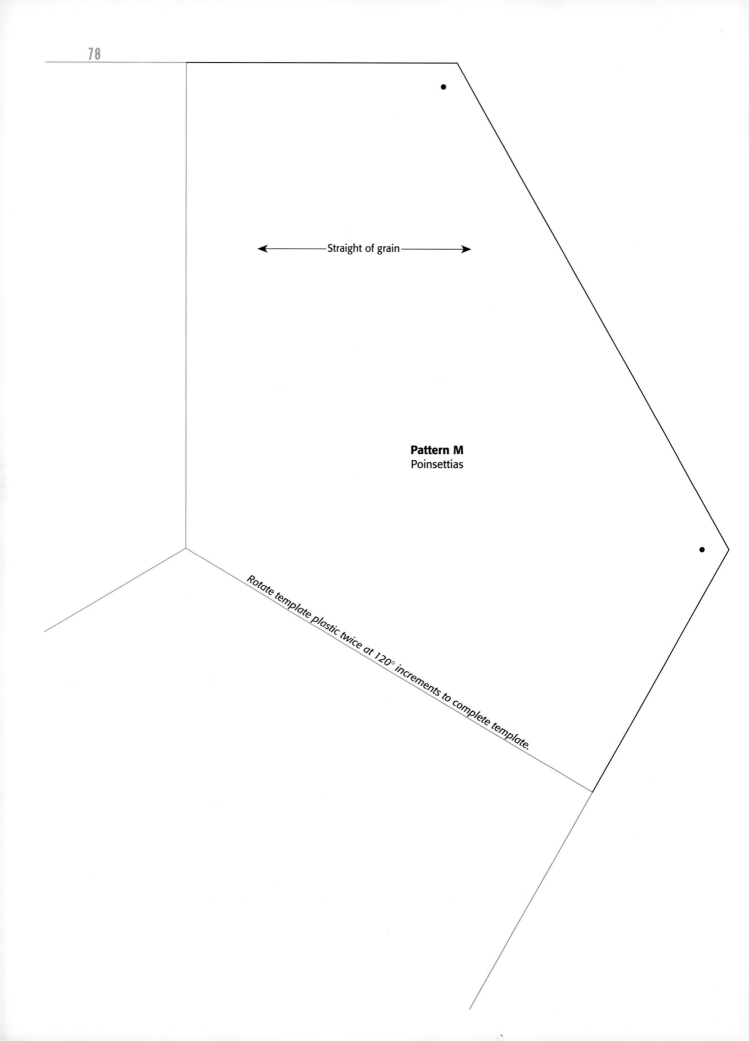

Straight of grain

Pattern M
Poinsettias

Rotate template plastic twice at 120° increments to complete template.

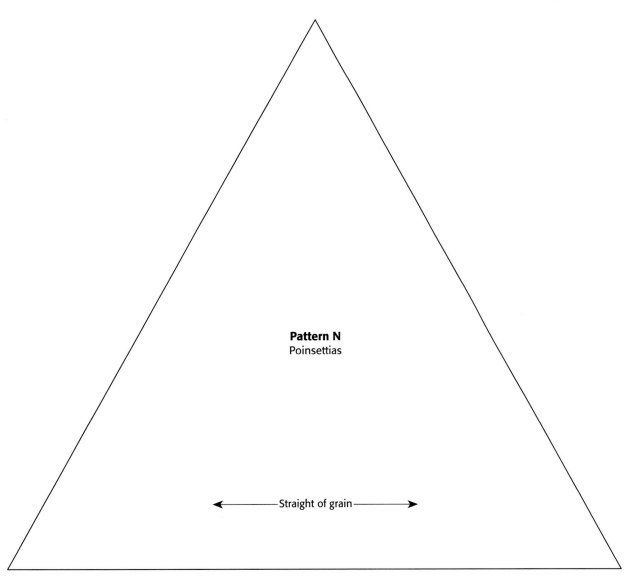

Pattern N
Poinsettias

←————Straight of grain————→

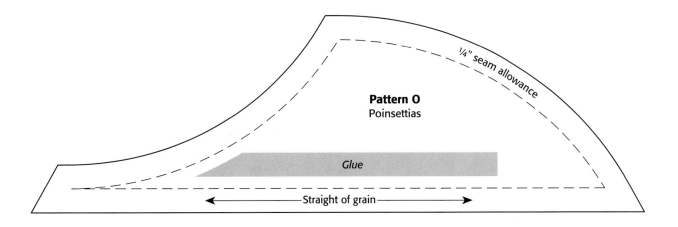

¼" seam allowance

Pattern O
Poinsettias

Glue

←————————Straight of grain————————→

About the Author

Martha Thompson earned a B.S. in home economics from Colorado State University in 1972, married her high school sweetheart, and began a family. She discovered quiltmaking in 1985 when a friend took her to visit the Nimble Thimble in Littleton, Colorado. By the next week she was working there.

Encouraged by the owner, Holly James, she studied every book on the shelves, attended a Mary Ellen Hopkins seminar, and became a prolific patchworker. Teaching came naturally. Then she discovered the Colorado Quilting Council, which opened up more doors and introduced her to a world of wonderfully creative and vibrant people. She had found her passion.

Square Dance was Martha's first book, published by That Patchwork Place in 1995. It is still in print and enjoyed by lovers of geometry and patchwork worldwide. Next came *Start with Squares,* a collection of quick-piecing techniques for scrap quilts. It is out of print, but its unusual designs and techniques live on in many classes and publications.

Four years ago Martha founded the Stone Soup Quilting Ministry to make and give big, warm quilts to adult patients of the Fred Hutchinson Cancer Research Center in Seattle, Washington. This ministry of compassion has delivered almost five hundred quilts and is still growing. She has developed a very successful model for organizing more than a hundred volunteer quilters into an ongoing ministry and is available for consultation.

Martha lives in Seattle with her husband of thirty years. They have two grown sons and one lovely daughter-in-law. She enjoys community service with the Multifaith AIDS projects. Martha is currently a graduate student of theology at Seattle University.